Raspberry Pi Programming Genius

How to Learn Python Easily & Manage Your Own Project

By: Jason Scotts

TABLE OF CONTENTS

Jason Scotts

PUBLISHERS NOTES
Disclaimer

This publication is intended to provide helpful and informative material. It is not intended to diagnose, treat, cure, or prevent any health problem or condition, nor is intended to replace the advice of a physician. No action should be taken solely on the contents of this book. Always consult your physician or qualified health-care professional on any matters regarding your health and before adopting any suggestions in this book or drawing inferences from it.

The author and publisher specifically disclaim all responsibility for any liability, loss or risk, personal or otherwise, which is incurred as a consequence, directly or indirectly, from the use or application of any contents of this book.

Any and all product names referenced within this book are the trademarks of their respective owners. None of these owners have sponsored, authorized, endorsed, or approved this book.

Always read all information provided by the manufacturers' product labels before using their products. The author and publisher are not responsible for claims made by manufacturers.

Paperback Edition 2013

Manufactured in the United States of America

DEDICATION

This book is dedicated to my parents who always encouraged me to live the dream.

Jason Scotts

CHAPTER 1- AN OVERVIEW OF RASPBERRY PI

When Raspberry Pi, the credit-card-sized single-board computer developed by the Raspberry Pi Foundation in the UK was launched, the concept of multi-purpose, light distribution platforms for promotion of teaching of basic computer science in schools was born. At present, Element 14/Premier Farnell and RS Components companies license sales of Raspberry Pi. The Raspberry Pi Foundation works actively toward innovation and integration of new hardware and software updates.

Raspberry Pi is programmed in Python programming language. One of the most standard programming codec's available, Python is used to create compatibility in operating systems, infrastructure and software programs used by Raspberry Pi. Python is a programming language that is fairly easy to learn. By creating classes of scripted code, concepts can be expiated in summary form so that programming results are accessible to conduct commands on the spot.

Online programming communities dedicated to creation of new software application as system (SaaS) are a central part of the knowledge sharing world Python programming for Raspberry Pi and its open source transformation. The Raspberry Pi platform supports integration with all of the major operating systems available in digital computer board based devices on the market, including is a cross-platform application Linux frameworks.

Features

Raspberry Pi is a Broadcom BCM2835 system on a chip (SoC) with an ARM1176JZF-S 700 MHz processor and VideoCore IV GPU. The current Raspberry Pi system is 512MB, upgraded from 256 megabytes of RAM. At present, the Raspberry Pi Foundation offers Arch Linux ARM and Debian distributions for download.

Architecture

Visual diagram of API connections in the Raspberry Pi utilizes Linux kernel-based operating systems. Raspbian is the Debian-based free operating system used to optimize Raspberry Pi hardware. The board's GPU hardware is accessed by way of a firmware image or binary blob; loaded into the GPU when booted from the SD-card. The firmware image is closed source at present.

The processing functions within the board's application software source run-time libraries to access an open source API driver, inside the Linux kernel. Video applications employing 2D and 3D applications, OpenMAX and OpenGL ES use OpenVG and EGL. The board's new proof of concept SD card image reinforces the preliminary operating system. The image can run in QEMU which enables Raspberry Pi to be mirrored on other platform architecture.

System Software

Raspberry Pi Fedora Remix software application is the one of the most recent developments for Linux distribution. The 2012 release was part of an ongoing effort in App exchange to upgrade efficiencies in the operating system. Systems software also includes Slackware ARM version 13.37. Free VideoCore driver code runs the Raspberry Pi ARM, is another example of open source multimedia SoC software available to the public.

Operating Systems

Raspberry Pi is compatible with a number of standard operating systems running that are ported or in the process of port integration. Operating systems compatibility includes cross platform applications frameworks developed for solely for Raspberry Pi's integration of Linux distribution.

Multi-purpose distributions in Moebius offer light ARM HF. Application of Moebius in Raspberry Pi is ostensible as it is small enough for 1GB SD memory. So minimal in memory usage, in fact, is Moebius that it optimizes the Raspberry Pi operating system with the least possible consumption. Finally,single purpose light distributions such as IPFire and Raspbmc are available for Raspberry Pi integration without additional programming.

User Applications

Raspberry Pi applications that can easily be installed on Raspbian involve multimedia, audio, graphics, Smartphone and LAN server functions. Open source media applications are built from outside sources to create new formats for unique user programming. Communities of programmers construct new software applications modules using the Python programming language, adding new information to dictionaries, lists and classes within the codec protocol.

Accessories

A prototype camera with 5 megapixels is set for release in April 2013. The module tested by the Foundation is one of the many accessory features Raspberry Pi supports. The board also interfaces with LEDs, analog signals, sensors, switches and other hardware devices, as well as an Arduino compatible controller.

Hardware

Schematics to both Raspberry Pi models (A and B) offer PCB connectors and ICs in block diagram. Model A does not include an internal connection to Ethernet. USB dongle can be employed to connect to external Ethernet. Model B contains an embedded Ethernet feature.

While Raspberry Pi Model A does not come with an Ethernet port, it can be connected to a network externally or by way of Wi-Fi adapter. There is no difference in performance between Model A and Model B in this regard, as internal Ethernet and external port connection offer

Jason Scotts

the same adaptation. Generic USB keyboards and mice are both compatible with Raspberry Pi.

Due to the fact that Raspberry Pi does not include a clock with auto recognition, the operating systems must be commanded to access a network time server. This can also be achieved by way of request for date stamping. Hardware accelerated video (H.264) encoding is also new. Two recent releases of codec's that can be integrated separately MPEG-2 and Microsoft's VC-1 increases the capabilities of video in Raspberry Pi.

Raspberry Pi is slated to support CEC which will allow for it to be controlled by way of television remote control. Other recent innovations include a revision 2.0 board in response to some minor update for corrections and improvement. Raspberry Pi Model B now has a larger memory with 512MB RAM chips.

CHAPTER 2- RASPBERRY PI- PYTHON- WHAT IS IT AND WHAT ARE THE BENEFITS?

Raspberry Pi is a credit card sized, single-board computer under innovation by the Raspberry Pi Foundation UK. The multi-purpose, light distribution platform is popular for teaching basic computer science in schools. The Raspberry Pi Foundation participates in the active development of Python programming language development of new hardware and software updates for its system.

Programming Raspberry Pi's Linux operating system (OS) and other software interface in Python programming language is the simplest codec for creating commands. Simple syntax in Python allows programmers to construct code with the minimal effort. The programming language deploys with concise concept statements over the more extensive scripting of programming languages.

Python Programming Language Proficiencies for Raspberry Pi

The high-level programming language, Python, is recognized as general purpose code. The code structure is used in Web programming language in 2.0. This allows cross-browser portability and aggregate exchange of data. The proficiency of Python's standard is now used in Web based software application as system (SaaS) platforms in support of data sharing platforms with Unicode. Raspberry Pi Python programming communities participate in open source sharing of software innovation.

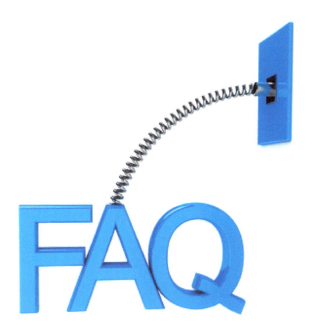

Online programming communities contributing to the development of new SaaS compatible with Raspberry Pi are important to the evolution of Python language libraries and codec found in open source sharing platforms. The Raspberry Pi platform offers a foundation for learning computer programming code standard to most operating systems (OS) on the market. This includes some of the systems cross-platform application Linux frameworks (i.e. Arch Linux ARM, Android, Android 4.0, Google Chrome OS, Chromium OS and Firefox OS).

Python multiple programming paradigms support constructs in programming Raspberry Pi compatible architecture, infrastructure software. The fact that Python allows for small and large coding structures to be constructed in commands provides the necessary functional, imperative and object-oriented programming elements to the various levels of software interface to the system.

The automatic memory management and fully dynamic type system in Python are the basis to the Raspberry Pi large library of coding language. Raspberry Pi is designed to integrate with other standard Linux platforms on the market. Python programming language can be deployed to command standalone executable programs with third-party tools, and is embedded in quite a few popular software applications.

Programming Raspberry Pi in Python

Python's multi-paradigm programming language enables Raspberry Pi programmers to conduct object-oriented programming and structured programming. The programming language also supports logic programming for extensions. Raspberry Pi's memory management is conducted by way of Python programming language using dynamic typing, reference counting and a cycle-detecting garbage collector features. Programmers will find that dynamic name resolution in Python serves to merge method and variable names upon execution of a program.

Python's syntax and semantics are highly readable and simple to replicate. The Python language syntax model results in uncluttered codecs. Future recognition of frequencies in scripting is part of the programming repository. In Python punctuation and syntactic exceptions are noticed. Semantic precision is derived from recognition, and exceeds that of alternate C or Pascal programming language. Python employs real language (and, or, not) for constructing boolean operators rather than symbols. Here are examples of Python programming language execution for Raspberry Pi: IDLE, Numbers, Variables, For Loops, Simulating Dice, If, While, Summary and Features.

Python expressions are much like those in C and Java programming language. Python converts expressions by truncating in response to comparative values. Object identification or comparative reference is also possible. Python implementation of object-orientation promotes segmentation programming of structure, so that each class is responsible for its own behavior. This modular approach to programming language assists in monitoring functions within the complexity of a program, making them far more manageable to administer.

Chaining comparative syntactic expressions creates series of commands. The mathematical formula to the chaining function is integer division. The integer division model is used to truncate the values. Conversion of one of the integers to a float is the result. The outcome to integer division model is, therefore, expressed in alpha form rather than numeric value.

Raspberry Pi libraries online containing Python programming language include a large repository of codecs for building programs. This includes modules applied with arithmetic arbitrary precision decimals, graphical user interface (GUI) programming, codecs for connecting relational databases, and codecs of regular expressions. Unit testing and software testing for Raspberry Pi in Python (i.e. doctest and unittest) modules is also available.

Although Raspberry Pi does not require a standard library for Python run or embed, there are a number of packages designed specifically for developer purposes (i.e. documentation tools, graphical user interface, image processing, multimedia, databases, networking and communications, scientific computing, text processing, web framework, and test frameworks and systems administration). Raspberry Pi programmers seeking library guidance for programming mathematical software in Python will find algebra, calculus, combinatorics, and numerical mathematic and number theory codecs. Strings and lists representing data can be used to add structure to Python based programs.

Integrating Raspberry Pi Hardware with Python

There are various methods of connecting Raspberry Pi to other electronic devices using GPIO Pin Connections. Programming in Python allows direct connection of GPIO Pins and extensions to supplement Raspberry Pi motherboard commands. The RaspiRobot also requires Python interface to control commands from a wireless USB keyboard to the motor in the robot chassis by way of ultrasonic range finder. This prototype invention is an example of a unique Raspberry Pi conversion project. Python programming language assists in rover command.

Jason Scotts

CHAPTER 3- THE BASICS OF PYTHON TECHNOLOGY

Python's high-level programming language is a general purpose code. Simple syntax enables programmers to create more limited code for the same concepts than is possible in other programming languages. Innovated in the 1980s, Python is the subsequent programming language to ABC. The programming language 2.0 was released by 2000. New features and support for Unicode promoted the efficacy of community knowledge sharing in development of programming code.

Python constructs support multiple programming paradigms for architecture, infrastructure, web based platforms and software. Small or large coding structures can be built into commands consistent with functional, imperative and object-oriented programming styles. Python's automatic memory management and fully dynamic type system allow for extensive derivation from a large repository of language.

Python is not restricted to scripting language, and can be packaged as part of standalone executable programs with third-party tools. Python interpretation is offered for most operating systems. The programming language is embedded in a number of popular software products on the market.

Python Features

The multi-paradigm programming language, Python allows for object-oriented programming and structured programming. The language features of the programming language can also support extensions including logic programming. The dynamic typing, reference counting and a cycle-detecting garbage collector features are exceptional for memory management. Dynamic name resolution serves to link method and variable names during execution of programs.

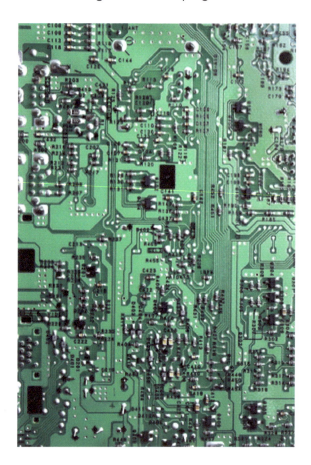

Python Syntax and Semantics

Python syntax and semantics are simple and highly readable for replication. The model of Python language syntax is uncluttered. Frequencies in language usage are retained in the repository of the programming language so that there is future recognition. Punctuation and syntactic exceptions are noted, making semantics even more precise in acknowledgement that alternate programming languages such as C or Pascal.

Python Expressions

Similar to C and Java programming expressions, Python conversion of expressions truncates by comparative value. Object identities or comparison by reference may also be used. Those comparisons can be chained to create a series of commands. Integer division is the model used to truncate values by converting one of the integers to a float. Due to the fact that Python used real language rather (and, or, not) for boolean operators rather than symbols, the result of the integer division model is still expressed in alpha form.

Python Libraries

The Python programming language has a sizable standard library for building programs. Standard internet formats and protocols MIME and HTTP are both supported. Other modules used for arithmetic with arbitrary precision decimals, creation of graphical user interfaces, connection to relational databases, and manipulation of regular expressions is available. Unit testing and software testing in the Python library in doctest and unittest modules performs reliability on new developments.

Although the standard library is not required to run or embed Python programming language in an application, the Python Package Index, the official repository of third-party software for the codecs, contains an extensive number of packages for developer purposes: scientific computing, text processing, image processing, graphical user interface, multimedia, databases, networking and communications, web framework, and test frameworks, documentation tools, system administration.

Python libraries such as Matplotlib, NumPy and SciPy enable the programming language to be applied efficiently in scientific computing. For instance, libraries used to program mathematical software in Python will be comprised of mathematical elements: algebra, calculus, combinatorics, numerical mathematic and number theory.

Python Software Development

The Python programming language is currently embedded in a number of popular software products. The use of Python scripting language with finite element method software like Abaqus or 3D animation software (i.e. Cinema 4D, Houdini, Lightwave, Maya, modo, MotionBuilder, Nuke and Softimage) and 2D imaging programs (i.e. GIMP, Inkscape, Paint Shop Pro and Scribus) is valued for its accessibility.

The use of complex structures like C++ containers in GNU GDB is evidence that Python is a sophisticated enough programming language to handle visual dynamics. It is also used for script writing of ArcGIS, video games, and as the language of choice for Web based update of platforms (i.e. Go, Google App Engine and Java).

Python Software Application as System (SaaS)

The fact that Python has been used as artificial intelligence in software application as system (SaaS) tasks makes it a preferred scripting language with module architecture. The rich text processing tools and syntax of Python are optimum for natural language processing. Its ready exploitation capabilities of almost any information security

Jason Scotts

infrastructure and application in targeted open source programming language development communities reveals the exceptional flexibility of the use of Python in any SaaS environment.

Web applications scripting interface with development of a standard API frameworks supports development of complex applications design and maintenance. For instance, Pyjamas and IronPython are client-side developers of Ajax-based applications. The popular SQLAlchemy used for data mapping of relational databases also uses Python programming language. It also supports the twisted framework designed to creating programming of communications between computers.

Python Developer Communities

The entrance of Python as a standard language in most Linux distributions has made it widely used in opens source operating systems applications (i.e. FreeBSD, NetBSD, OpenBSD, OS X etc.). Installers for Linux distribution are also programmed in Python. Free and open source CPython software is proffered by way of a knowledge sharing exchange activity. The CPython online community development model allows iteration or completely new implementations of programming and sharing. CPython is a program of the Python Software Foundation. The Raspberry Pi Foundation's single-board computer project adopted Python codecs for its interface.

CHAPTER 4- OTHER GADGETS THAT CAN BE USED WITH RASPBERRY PI PYTHON

Before even getting into what other forms of technology can be connected to the Raspberry Pi it must be highlighted that the debut of this mini personal computer has created quite a storm in the information technology industry and has created a new wave of competition.

The benefits of the raspberry Pi are many the most advantageous being its size (it is the same size as a credit card). It has similar functions to a standard computer and is more cost effective. The possibility also exists to operate it as a low cost server that can deal with a bit of web or internal traffic. In the short and long term putting together a number of Raspberry Pi to create a server costs much less than getting a standard server. If the web traffic is light then a Raspberry Pi can be used and money can be saved.

Jason Scotts

Since I have become familiar with the Pi technology I have conducted a few experiments of my own with a number of sensors and other devices. From these experiments I have put together a list of the devices that I have found to work rather well with this type of technology. The items do not cost a lot and integrate easily with the software and can be the groundwork for an even bigger project.

The items that can be created range from security systems to robot cars and can be put together in a number of ways to make something fantastic. If you are buying a gift for a Raspberry Pi aficionado then this chapter will give you quite the head start on the selections that are available.

The first item that we can look at is the PIR movement sensor. It is a great piece of technology that allows the user to detect movement through the use of passive infra red sensors. These sensors are not costly and come with pins that can be connected right to the GPIO header of the Raspberry Pi. It is a great device to make a robotic sensor or to use with a security system.

The next item that can be looked at is the Nintendo Wii controller. This is a great option for the game lovers. The Wiimote can be connected to the raspberry Pi and open up a world of great possibilities as it pertains to gaming.

After that there is the ultrasonic module. These modules can improve the distance that can be read by the Raspberry Pi device. You can opt for an ultrasonic module that has an echo pin, a trigger pin and two power pins.

The next great item is the USB to serial module. This type of technology allows the Raspberry Pi to work on a USB interface. This USB can be plugged into a tablet, laptop or PC and then the pins can be connected to the Pi device.

The great thing is that the pins default settings can be a serial terminal interface than can be used from a tablet or PC to access Linux command. The possibility also exists to provide power for the Pi from the device that it is plugged into if there is enough power to support it.

Not to be left out is the Wi-Fi Dongle (USB). Again these are cheap and if you hate cables work well to help the user to connect the Pi to a network. One of the options that are extremely easy to configure using Wi-Fi technology is the Edimax 7811.

The USB Bluetooth Dongle is another great techie option. These can be bought online or in a computer store. This device allows you to make a connection with a number of Bluetooth devices like Wii controllers, computer mice and keyboards.

The character LCD display (16×2 or 20×4) is the next top option that can be looked at. These displays can be either 20 characters or 16 characters and are not hard to connect to the raspberry Pi's GPIO pins. All that you have to ensure when you are making your purchase is that the items are compatible. To be able to turn the screen on or off and to make adjustments to the brightness the user would only require a few more simple components.

Sticking to screens that work well with the Pi device, mini LCD screens can also be considered. There are quite a number of these screens that can accommodate a video input of a composite nature. These work well if the aim is to connect it to the Pi's video output. These screens are typically outfitted with two video inputs, come with 12 V power and are more often than not used as reversing camera screens for cars.

Now we can look at LED buzzer boards. The one that will be focused on is the BerryClip 6 LED board. It can be plugged right into the Pi's GPIO header and is considered and add on board. With this device the user will have a momentary switch, a buzzer and 6 LEDS that are colored. Any language can be used to control then and one can simply look through the various Python scripts to find a suitable one.

Last but not least there is the stepper motor. The one that I tried had a controller board that could be connected directly to the Pi's GPIO. All the user has to do is put in a series of sequences and the motor will turn.

CHAPTER 5- USING RASPBERRY PI TO CREATE AN LED INDICATOR

The Raspberry Pi is the ideal piece of equipment to use to connect an indicator light for a myriad of projects like new mails or weather notifications. This chapter will highlight the way that this can be done.

Some may wonder why something like this would even be considered. The real deal is that it is a fun project to undertake.

As highlighted in the previous chapter the Raspberry Pi is something that you can do a lot of experiments with and learn something new at the end of the day. No one really needs a device to indicate whether it is going to rain or not but it really is a fun project to work on.

What Is Needed To Do This?

Jason Scotts

If you opt not to follow the tutorial you will require a few things. The assumption in this case is that you are already knowledgeable on the basics of Raspberry Pi and can install Raspbian on the Raspberry Pi.

Apart from having a Pi unit that not only works effectively but has Raspbian installed on it you will require some more items. You will need:

1 raspberry pi case (clear)

1 ledborg module

One thing to bear in mind is that the choice of case if optional as to whether you want it to be frosted or clear. If the case you currently have is opaque you will have to make adjustments to it by either using a breakout kit with GPIO extension or simply cutting a hole in the case so the LED indicator can be seen. The breakout kit, though it will bring the cost on material purchases up a bit will be more beneficial for any customizations you will do in the end. You will have a greater ability to place the Led under something to illuminate it or inside something to do same.

Getting the LedBorg Installed

Though, if you are up to it you can put build an LED indicator, you can find some pretty cost effective ones like the LedBorg to purchase.

It is pretty easy to get the module installed and the design allows it to be set right on the Raspberry Pi GPIO pins. To stat you need to shut down the Pi and then open the case.

Before getting started it is essential that the module be oriented so that the LedBorg icon is close to RCA module. In a nutshell the edges of the Pi board should be flush with the LedBorg and the overhang should not be over the edge but only hanging over the Pi board.

With the Pi board open, it is the perfect time to cover the Led indicators that are beside the USB ports especially if a clear case is being used. This will help avoid the confusion with reading the LedBorg indicator as the network indicator lights and power lights tend to be rather bright.

A simple solution is to cover the lights with electrical tape (white). It will reduce the brightness of the lights so they can be still be seen but not detract from the LedBorg.

As soon as the LedBorg is correctly installed and all other adjustments are mad the case can be closed. Before moving on to the next phase, turn the Pi back on and let it boot up.

Installing the Software

First one has to find a suitable software package that come with the requisite drivers which allow access to the LedBorg from the command line and also has a GUI controller. Just ensure that whichever package you select is compatible with the Raspberry Pi board that you have and the version of Raspbian that you have installed.

If your Raspberry Pi has mounting holes then there is certain procedure that you have to follow and if it has none then there is another procedure that you will have to follow. These are thing with which you would already be familiar. You will also have to be aware of the Raspbian kernel version. To do a quick check all you have to do is open the terminal up and enter the command uname-r to do a quick check.

Jason Scotts

As soon as you have all the information, you can proceed to the next step and get the link for your package. For the purposes of example the Revision 1 board is being used with the 3.6.11 kernel.

To get the installation process underway the terminal on the Raspberry Pi needs to be opened. Once this is done a series of commands can be entered to get the package installed. Keep in mind that the third command URL has to be replaced with the board/kernel package URL.

When this point is reached then you will have the drivers and GUI wrapper installed. When you look on the Raspbian desktop an icon will be there for the GUI wrapper.

You can proceed by launching the GUI wrapper. To do this, simply click the Led Borg icon. This is the time that you can check to ensure that the module is working properly. You can select any color and save it to try it out.

In the demo mode you are able to go through the range of colors and you can see them at various speeds. You can also see how they work at low output and high output.

It is here that you also have the option to configure the LedBorg. You can simply go to the colors section of the CPU and the Led will first be green then yellow and then be red. This merely indicates the ARM processors load. It is best to change the speed to slow as this will be more beneficial in the long run.

Apart from that you can also use RGB values to select the colors as opposed to using the GUI interface alone.

CHAPTER 6- RASPBERRY PI PYTHON- GRAPHICAL USER INTERFACES

Programming Raspberry Pi for graphical user interfaces (GUI) with Python programming language can be best managed by event handler functions. GUI programs are event-driven means that code in the event handlers may not be called directly by the program without triggers. This makes Python handy for creating GUI program management. Use Python to trigger the event handler so the other elements of the program read code, call other functions or change variables accordingly. Since the event handler is not called by code but by triggered response, variables cannot be passed in correspondence with event handler parameters in the program. Global variables offer the trigger for using a class in Python to activate GUI event handling for Raspberry Pi.

GUI Development in Python

Jason Scotts

Applications embedded with the Python programming language are many. There are currently a number of popular software application products on the market using the Python codec for scripting language. Python also allows for object-oriented and structured command coding. The use of Python programming language for GUI in Raspberry Pi reveals the extent by which new innovations in graphics software programs can be customized. For programmers learning how to script code and object-oriented event handler triggers for GUI, Python is the optimum choice.

Python provides finite method to software development of GUI programs like Abaqus and 3D animation software (i.e. Maya, Cinema 4D, Lightwave, modo, Houdini, MotionBuilder, Nuke and Softimage) as well as 2D imaging programs (i.e. Inkscape, GIMP, Paint Shop Pro and Scribus). Unlike the use of complex structures seen in C++ programming language containers deployed in GNU GDB Python is exceptionally simple and sophisticated to handle almost any programming language applied to visual dynamics. Python is seen in the scripting of ArcGIS and video game programming language, as well as in the development of new Web based apps platforms (i.e. Go, Google App Engine and Java).

Programming GUI with Python

Python's classes and object-oriented programming are sufficient basis for class definition of objects and running code. Data variables are part of a class. Definition of data that can be used within an object is created by class. Class is the definitive function for object-oriented application of data. When data variables are outside the object, they are denoted as fields. Functions in this realm supply methods for manipulation of data. Data fields define event handlers, which access any data required for trigger. Image conversion is done to a canvas. Image constructs are added to the dictionary for later use.

Python's dictionary enables for built-in types to be accessed later. When programming GUI in Raspberry Pi with Python, there are four (4) collections used: 1) string, 2) tuple, 3) list and 4) dictionary. Programming languages typically string text to form a series in a collection. Python is modular in the sense that segmentation of the collection applies to string statements as well. Consideration of a tuple as a group of objects is the function for a list. Tuples and strings are unchangeable. Lists may be changed, however, and this is normally done by sorting or appended logic within a series. The individual elements of strings, tuples and lists are available in numeric indices. Much like lists, dictionaries in Python are highly mutable. Dictionary indices provide a guide to application. Python library support for classes is available in documentation.

Using Tkinter for programming GUI for Raspberry Pi in Python

Tkinter offers the binding importation of Python programming of GUI in Raspberry Pi. Tkinter Tk GUI toolkit is the de facto standard used by Python to program code in Raspberry Pi, as well as Windows and Mac OS X. Tk bindings are implemented as a Python wrapper. The wrapper surrounds the complete Tcl interpreter embedded in a Python interpreter. Calls in Tkinter 1) translate to Tcl commands, 2) fed to the embedded interpreter and 3) merge Python and Tcl into a single application. Both Python 2.7 and Python 3.1 incorporate the functionality of Tk 8.5, so that Tk widgets can be themed to appear as a native desktop environment where the application is running.

Extension of a class is acknowledged as inheritance within Python programming language. The transition of class to inheritance is a

Jason Scotts

fundamental aspect of object-oriented programming for GUI in Raspberry Pi with Python codecs. When functions of Tk are made relevant to a class, extension of the class can be made to add as much content in programming language as desired. Classes also can be used to define initialize (__init__) which is a special function command. When this is applied the class is relevant to creation of an object.

An easy way to initialize in GUI, definition of statements should be programmed by indenting those statements within the class level to create new commands. If the first parameter to special commands is 'self'; how the various parts of the class recognize each other is formed. This is done to segment the logic inside of a class. Once global variables are created as fields in a class, the definition of event handlers as part of the class can be programmed. By defining the class needed to create the object that will be active an object app from the class must be articulated in relation to a parent name. Top level windows have no parents. Creation of an object to commence event initialization processing in Tk is done by calling the __init__ function to form a complete main loop().

CHAPTER 7- RASPBERRY PI- HOW TO USE PYGAME

To create a game in Pygame on the Raspberry Pi, one will need to work in conjunction with the Geany Editor to code the game. The first thing that one can do is to open the Geany Editor on their computer so that they may create a new template. Upon opening a new template file, some code will need to be input to instruct Geany to use the Python coding language as well as a basic template code.

Pygame might not always be installed so if it's not, the person can open a terminal and type "sudo apt-get install python-pygame" without the quotations. Upon entering the root password, the Pygame package and dependencies will be downloaded, extracted and installed.

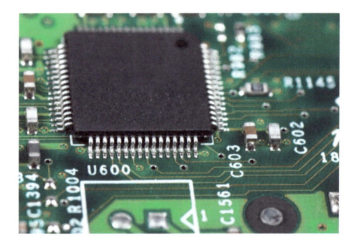

Creating a simple application that displays a window and has minimal event handling properties is ideal for someone learning how to use Pygame for the first time. After successfully learning some basic coding and programming for game coding in Pygame, one will be able to try their hand at more advanced types of games.

The first thing that one will need to do is to instruct the Geany program which coding language they would like to use. This can be done by entering "#! /usr/bin/env python" without quotations into line 1. Line 2 may be left blank and line 3 should have the text "import pygame". The line of text "import pygame" will import the PyGame module which is needed to code and program games. Line 4 may also be left blank; meanwhile line 5 should have the text "screen = pygame.display.set_mode ((640, 400))" without quotations. This code instructs the PyGame module what size measurements to set the display screen.

The following line 6 should also be left blank while line 7 should contain the text "while 1:" without quotations. Lastly, "pass" should be input into line 8. One may experiment by running this code by clicking on the small rotating gears icon to initialize the code start.

Upon executing the code, the individual will be greeted by a graphical display window with size dimensions of 640 by 400 pixels. Once the individual has successfully coded a graphical window, they may experiment with different size dimensions for the window if they desire.

The next step is to add an event loop to the program code that will continue to loop until the user utilizes the poll which in turn changes the event to the next event in the event queue. Next, the person may add some code to the program to allow for the end-user to close the graphical display window by clicking on the display window exit button.

To do this, further code must be entered to instruct a flag to run the event loop until the poll method has been used to change events. In line 6, the code "running = 1" should be entered without quotations. Line 7 should be left blank and line 8 should have the text "while running:" input.

Line 9 contains the the code to instruct the Pygame module of the event poll. The code that should be input is "event = pygame.event.poll()" without the quotations. Line 10 should have "if event.type == pygame.QUIT:" entered and line 11 should have "running = 0" entered without the quotations.

Once the code is ran, a graphical display window will open and the user may click on the exit button on the window to close it. Alternatively, the individual may also leave the running flag out of the code so that there is not a programming loop. Once the basis code has been programmed, the individual may configure the window template to enable smooth transitioning between windows and also to change the colors of the window itself.

In line 12, the following text should be entered: "screen.fill((0, 0, 0))" and in line 13, the following text should be entered: "pygame.display.flip()" without the quotations. This will set the background screen color on the graphical display window as well as allow for smooth animations between window changes.

The background values of 0, 0, 0 represent the values for red, blue and green. With values set to 0,0,0 a black screen will be displayed; however the values may be changed as the individual wishes from anywhere from 0 to 255.

Jason Scotts

Once the color values have been set to what the user desires, they may go ahead and program code to create an invisible buffer. This invisible buffer is used to draw on rather than directly onto the screen. After the drawing has been finished, the buffer layer may be set to invisible. When this is done correctly, animations will transitions smoothly instead of flickering.

Alternatively, one can also sample some coding exercises to display the color of the time of day it is. For example, the individual may code their program to analyze the time and display a color corresponding to the time of day. One may select a different color for each time period of the day for the graphical window to display.

Upon practicing these basic exercises that include event handles and running flags, one will soon be able to progress their skills and techniques when using Pygame. However, it is essential that one understands how to use basic features of the Pygame module before attempting to progress. This will ensure that the person understands the basic code strings, what they do and how to edit their program properly.

CHAPTER 8- NETWORKING WITH RASPBERRY PI PYTHON

Raspberry Pi networking by way of both Model A and Model B versions of the computer device can be done by traditional Ethernet or WiFi. While Model B comes wired for Ethernet, Model A requires an external port support by way of USB 2.0. The Ethernet option is not a Gigabit Ethernet supported feature. WiFi can be connected via standard USB in both versions with upstream bandwidth reception. At this time, Raspberry Pi systems require USB dongles to connect to the internet.

Raspberry Pi networking capabilities are performed by a Broadcom BCM2835 system on a chip (SoC) with an ARM1176JZF-S 700 MHz processor. ARM Linux WiFi is not entirely sufficient at this time. Connecting more than two USB devices can be done by utilizing a hub to add more ports. Some Raspberry Pi keyboards have had hubs built-in. This makes this option quite flexible. Most IT specialists working with Raspberry Pi recommend powered hub support. Raspberry Pi uses Linux as the server. Connection to the internet can be accessed remotely with a static IP address. Broadband connection of an IP to a Raspberry Pi computer network can be done by way of router.

Instructions to networking Raspberry Pi in Debian Linux

Instructions to Raspberry Pi running Debian Linux for network connectivity is discretionary to the Linux supported interface, but is parallel to other distributions available on the market. Linux requests a dynamic IP addressed whenever a router issues connection. Static connection requires an address that is unchanged, 192.168.1.4. This is in the case that a LAN is available, rather than WiFi.

By locating the DHCP address with the ifconfig command, Ethernet protocols to the port address mentioned can be performed. A router command is also required. Find the destination and gateway to show the router IP address. Traffic is sent via the router to the gateway. There will also be an address range issued by the router, and this is unique to individual router protocol. LAN settings, router address and any DHCP requests are provided entries between a range of addresses for the server. Alternately, a static IP address can be sought, again by way of the server address and gateway for initiation of the connection.

Source the name server entry correspondent to the default gateway or direct to the ISP name servers. Dynamic reload of a network interface can be conducted with reboot to verify source of configuration is correct. Networking commands to make changes to dynamic network configurations apply the 'ipconfig' command to activate or deactivate the online interface. Another option is to use 'ifup' or 'ifdown' commands for error record details.

Raspberry Pi Programming Genius

Six (6) Steps to Networking Raspberry Pi

Here is a tutorial on how to set up a wireless networking capability in Raspberry Pi. Networking options increase access to new Python generated libraries for programming Web based software applications. This includes software applications as system (SaaS) that perform infrastructural operations. With so much to gain in terms of operating systems, knowledge sharing and programming language codecs online, networking is by far the optimum connection to advancement of the Raspberry Pi community's joint efforts in programming excellence.

By plugging in a wireless device into Raspberry Pi or a USB hub on the computer, the machine is prepared to receive the commands for networking connectivity

Find out the name of the device, so that protocols to the necessary drivers can be mapped out prior to issuing request for internet support.

$ lsusb is the syntax for sourcing all USB devices within a Raspberry Pi platform. Review the USB record for a file that represents the wireless device. Find a wireless adapter in the USB device list. Sample result to this search will index the key device ID information required for the drivers (i.e. bus port no., manufacturing no., serial no. etc.).

Package information must be updated prior to creating a network. Source udpates from Debian by entering '$ apt-get update', and enter '$ apt-cache search RTL818' once the download as finished. A device ID may be different than is required for recognition. Some programmers recommend shortening the ID description. The goal is to locate the adapter by using the apt-cache command in this manner. Enter the command to find the proper adapter on the USB port list: '$ lsmod'. The same ID should show up.

Jason Scotts

Generate a file (configuration) for the wireless adapter by entering the command: '$ sudo nano /etc/wpa.config'. Save the file and go back to the $prompt for network commands. This will lead to the final step in confirmation to add a location to the interfaces.

The final step in the process is unplugging the network cable to test the wireless device for aptitude. Restart the network by entering: '$ sudo /etc/init.d/networking restart' to complete.

Networking connectivity of Raspberry Pi to online communities has led to profound changes in open source applications interests. The development of Python programming language to support Raspberry Pi programming activities is seen in innovations in online social networking platform integrations with social media sites and other community groups dedicated to the development of Raspberry Pi and Python networking activities.

For more information about networking Raspberry Pi with Python programming language codecs, source Python libraries for details about dictionaries, lists, modules and classes applied in scripting connectivity of Raspberry Pi with external devices and Web based applications. Raspberry Pi supports multi-scale interfaces compatible with cross-platform application Linux frameworks and operating systems.

ABOUT THE AUTHOR

Jason Scotts was always encouraged to take a keen interest in a variety of topics from an early and with this encouragement he started to find out as much as he could about topics that he was interested in.

He had a keen interest in technology from an early age and as such made it a point of duty to read about any new form of technology that comes out.

The aim that Jason has is to inform and educate. He is not forcing the information on anyone but leaves them to make an informed decision at the end of text as to whether or not they want to try this form of technology.

Jason is aware that though the wheels of technology are turning and many new technologies are being released not many individuals are up to date and he uses his books to help update those who are a bit behind.

www.ingramcontent.com/pod-product-compliance
Lightning Source LLC
Chambersburg PA
CBHW041147050326
40689CB00001B/518